YOUR KNOWLEDGE HAS VALUE

Bibliographic information published by the German National Library:

The German National Library lists this publication in the National Bibliography; detailed bibliographic data are available on the Internet at http://dnb.dnb.de .

Imprint:

Copyright © 2016 GRIN Verlag, Open Publishing GmbH
Print and binding: Books on Demand GmbH, Norderstedt Germany
ISBN: 9783668228757

This book at GRIN:

http://www.grin.com/en/e-book/322771/audience-and-empathy-film-as-a-uniquely-evocative-medium

Timothy McGlinchey

Audience and Empathy. Film as a Uniquely Evocative Medium

GRIN Publishing

GRIN - Your knowledge has value

Since its foundation in 1998, GRIN has specialized in publishing academic texts by students, college teachers and other academics as e-book and printed book. The website www.grin.com is an ideal platform for presenting term papers, final papers, scientific essays, dissertations and specialist books.

Visit us on the internet:

http://www.grin.com/

http://www.facebook.com/grincom

http://www.twitter.com/grin_com

Table of Contents

Audience and Empathy: Film as a Uniquely Evocative Medium

Introduction

An individual's capacity to not only acknowledge, but rather share and vicariously experience the emotions of another, is a truly remarkable psychological phenomenon. This process of empathy, as it is above defined, is especially intriguing once removed from the context of human interaction, and in fact recognised within the seemingly disconnected dynamic of the fictional film viewing experience. Despite the appearance of what many may consider limitations to empathy in film viewing, such as the audience's knowledge of the inauthentic, staged nature of the medium, it remains clear that filmic narratives can still be affectively experienced by their viewers. As Metz remarks:

> More than the other arts, or in a more unique way, the cinema involves us in the imaginary: it drums up all perception, but to switch it immediately over into its own absence, which is nonetheless the only signifier present. (1982:45)

Taking this into consideration, this project seeks to scrutinise empathy's role in the film viewing experience with a focus on emotional response, whilst specifically investigating its impact in the context of fiction film. And so raises the primary research question: To what extent, and how, is fictional film capable of eliciting emotion in its audience?

In recognising the breadth of this topic and the complexity of its key themes, several other questions arise that must inevitably be addressed: how is emotional response measured and its causes identified? What are the barriers to affective response? What impact does subjectivity and

1

individual interpretation have on empathy and the viewer's reactions to film? What barriers and limitations may exist which could influence the affective response to film? Throughout this project the answers to these questions, and many others, will become pivotal to a reliable response to the overarching research questions.

Methodology

Both empathy and affect, as concepts, carry with them a degree of ambiguity regarding definition and the criteria by which they are determined or measured. This is of course problematic when considering the research process involved in this project which relies so heavily on the identification of them both. It is therefore crucial that the chosen methodological approaches offer depth and rigour, to the furthest extent possible. In this case, the methodology will include a screening, questionnaires given both before and after the film, and finally a focus group.

The film that was screened, *Pay It Forward* (Leder, 2000) follows a young boy, Trevor, who is given an assignment by his teacher to put into action an idea that can make a positive impact on the world. Meanwhile, he himself is coping with serious family difficulties including an alcoholic mother and absent father. Though an ultimately uplifting story which reinforces the goodness in people, it tragically ends with Trevor being killed trying to rescue his friend. It is primarily for its emotional appeal that this was chosen. There were six participants who took part in the screening, and because the project does not specifically focus on the impact of gender, age, or any other distinguishing categories, they were chosen at random. The questionnaires they were given before the screening were designed to gauge each participant's general viewing habits and preference for film genre, as such factors could influence the interpretation of data. After the screening, they were presented with one more questionnaire which asked more specific, quantitative questions regarding

2

the movie they had just watched. However, as Kumar (2005) rightly explains, questionnaires on their own do not provide respondents with the opportunity to clarify the questions asked of them, nor fully elaborate in the answers they give. With this in mind, a focus group was arranged which, in this case, was incredibly beneficial in its capacity to provide a thorough level of detail to each participant's response to the film, as well as contextualise their questionnaire answers.

Literature Review and Project Outline

Before delving into the outline of this project and its supporting academic basis, it is first beneficial to appreciate the degree of interest this general topic has generated:

> Ancient questions as to how and why it is that we can respond emotionally to characters and event which we know to be fictional, and whether it is rational to do so, have in recent years resurfaced and been at the heart of a debate as lively as any in contemporary aesthetics, a debate which continues to fill the pages of philosophical journals but which has so far resulted in little agreement even about the nature of the problems involved, let alone their solutions. (Neill, 1996:175)

Although the notable scope of interest and range of response to this topic can appear intimidating, it is also of benefit to have access to a broad range of perspectives, and from a variety of disciplines. At this early stage, a reflection on the emotive nature of art in general could offer valuable insight into the field and study of most interest in this project; film and audience studies. Swanger's (1993) description of how art provokes empathy in an individual can be similarly likened to the traits within film that achieve the same effect in a viewer:

Art, intent on the actualization of aesthetic vision, is devoted also to heightening feeling, whether it be feeling for a character in a novel or the feelings occasioned by a string quartet. Additionally, one of the feelings that art engenders is that of empathy; successful art creates a connection between the percipient's sensibility, the sensibility of the artist, and, if the art is representational, figures within it. (Swanger 1993:43)

A further advantage of being involved in a topic so far reaching, is that often one discipline's specific concern is even approached by another. For example, Stoller (1989) applies an anthropological perspective to the study of affect in film, and so looks at the issue differently. He explains; "[f]ilm can be a powerfully evocative medium, projecting to an audience a narrative which may be infused with sensual sights and sounds" (Stoller 1989:153). This quote highlights the aesthetic and sensory element involved in the affective response, whilst from the film studies perspective, Plantinga (2006) refers more to the content and substance of film:

If our goal is to understand how mainstream viewers experience films, if we want to explore the cultural role of movies, if we wish to expand our conception of the poetics of the cinema, then we cannot ignore the place of emotion elicitation and affective experience within film viewing. (Plantinga 2006:81)

As will become clearer throughout this project, the accessibility to such a diverse range of perspectives can only benefit the cause of the researcher who seeks a holistic understanding of the subject. That is not to say in this case, however, that the discipline of film studies itself does not offer its own wealth of contribution. With regards to the cause of the affective response to film, a process that occupies and drives this project's core debate, a range of interpretations can be found which fosters a critical and careful approach to generalisations. For example, Friedberg (1990)

4

emphasises the importance that empathy and identification has in fiction as it "conceals or defers the recognition of dissimilitude" (1990:40). Carroll, however, a key figure to this research investigation, argues against the process of "character-identification" and empathy altogether by claiming that there is often asymmetry between the feelings of an actor and the feelings of the observer. Instead, he advocates the concept of sympathy as a more suitable alternative.

And so, having explored only a fraction of the dense academic field that concerns itself with such topics as those discussed within, it is important to now begin aligning the knowledge this field offers to the key questions of this research project. In doing so, the intention is to define and elucidate the relationship between affect and empathy, in order to understand better the complex dynamics of the film-viewing experience.

Through its unique capacity to communicate and captivate, film has expanded beyond a mere representation of reality to become an expressive art form which offers its viewers an emotive and personal experience, forged through imagination whilst demanding it also. It is this emotive experience that inspires the central discussion of this project, and introduces the concept of empathy as its potential counterpart. However, in the early stages of this research, there were two assumptions made about the dynamics of film-viewing and audience response that have since become questionable. The first is that empathy, as a concept, is broad enough to solely account for the startling array of affective responses that viewers express towards fictional film. And the second is that the divide between real-world and fiction, for the viewer, is necessarily significant enough to warrant, or even require, a different set of human emotive processes than those most naturally found in real-world relationships. After reflection upon primary research findings which resulted from a film screening, focus group and questionnaires, as well as careful consideration of the relevant academic support this topic has accrued, it has become problematic to attend to such assumptions. It is therefore the intention of this project to elucidate those areas which prove challenging in the face of contradiction, whilst also providing a solution which recognises the importance of empathy as contributory to affective response, but favours a relational approach when acknowledging the topic in its full context.

Is Empathy Enough?

The most appropriate way to begin this discussion of empathy, given its contentious and ambiguous nature, is to prescribe it a definition to be applied as a measure of discrepancy. As Basch (1983) aptly remarks; "The word empathy sometimes means one thing, sometimes another, until now it does not mean anything" (1983:357). It is therefore for the sake of uniformity that one definition will be considered, which in this case, is an adaption of a contribution from the *Merriam-Webster Dictionary* (2015): the feeling of understanding and vicariously sharing another person's experiences and emotions. It is this definition that will facilitate the following discussion, as it is considered alongside the phenomenon that is brought about through an individual's affective response to fictional film.

As referred to in this project's methodology, emotion elicitation through film is considered by many, including Plantinga (2006:81), a core feature and goal of the film-going experience. However, it is this study's focus, as it is Neill's (1996), to ask the specific questions of "how and why it is that we can respond emotionally to characters and events which we know to be fictional, and whether it is rational to do so" (1996:175). Thus, the topic of empathy is introduced as a means of explaining this curious form of human expression, and the most basic reasoning behind doing so lies in its inherent vicarious nature. Neill's (ibid) initial argument for the worth of an empathy-driven theory originates beyond the field of film studies and enters into a breadth of other disciplines. He explains that a growing number of philosophers and psychologists are favouring the case of empathy in explaining our general ability to understand, explain and predict the behaviours of others (1996:178). The argument is then made that if it is indeed so prevalent in our everyday lives, should it not too impact our response to characters and plots of fiction. It is here that the findings from this project's primary research become valuable.

Neill (ibid) refers to the film *Don't Look Now* (Roeg, 1973) to illustrate empathy's role in the reception of fiction. In the film, the protagonist becomes involved with two psychics who claim they can communicate with her recently deceased daughter. The claim is made, in reference to this plot, that if the viewer could not relate to the protagonist, and in some way feel and identify with her pain of loss and desire for connection with her daughter, then they could in turn not relate to the entire plot which entails the belief in the supernatural (1996:181-182). Interestingly, in the focus group discussion as part of this research, a similar notion was echoed by several participants. The conversation revolved around the potential difficulties in accepting a plot which strongly contradicted a viewer's understanding of reality, and the film *Toy Story* was the subject of debate. It was at this point one participant, Megan, remarked; "I think the emotions the toys have are real. I think that's what makes it real". Her point being, even though the plot was so inconsistent with her knowledge of the world, she could relate to the actions and emotions of the main characters and subsequently accept the plot. If the term empathy is used in a similar way to the notion of identification, then it does seem apparent that relating to characters in an empathetic way is a fundamental element of the film-viewing experience. In fact, Friedberg (1990) refers to identification as "that which conceals or defers the recognition of dissimilitude" (1990:40), which is in keeping with both Megan's remark, and indeed a crucial point to Neill's (1996) argument.

However, it must be stated that this process of identification cannot be considered the direct cause of an emotional response, but rather, a contribution to the openness of the viewer to the plot and characters. In turn, the underlying process of empathy must also be challenged in its supposed capacity to incite an affective reaction. Carroll (1990) posits a convincing argument through the close examination of the limits of empathy's definition, by referring to its requisite for the vicarious sharing of the emotions or feelings of another. He illustrates his point with the following analogy:

> When the heroine is splashing about with abandon as, unbeknownst to her, a killer shark is zooming in for the kill, we feel concern for her. But that is not what she is feeling. She's feeling delighted. (1990:90)

To expand, Carroll (ibid) suggests that often the emotional reaction of a film viewer is not a vicarious mirroring of the character's, but something else entirely. It is this revelation that originally cast doubt on the assumption that empathy could account for the variety of affective response to film, as it alone appears to be insufficient. This was also demonstrated in the response of participants to the tragic death of Trevor, the protagonist in *Pay It Forward* (2000), the film screened as part of this research project. Two attendants in fact began to cry when Trevor died, whilst Trevor himself was not expressing sadness, nor were the other characters present in the scene who were either afraid or distressed. And so, if the limitations of empathy cannot be reconciled with the reality of audience response to fictional film, then either those limitations ought to be reconsidered, or alternative explanations explored.

Stotland (1969), for example, provides a definition of empathy that both allows for a varied emotional response to a singular stimulus, as well as flexibility in the arrival of said response (1969:272). To elaborate with reference to an example, in Carroll's analogy of the woman and the predator shark, Stotland might argue that the viewer could empathetically feel and express fear despite the character only expressing delight, and furthermore, that fear response could precede the inevitable stimulus; the shark attack. However, in this case the criteria for an empathetic response is arguably so distant from a uniform understanding, like that provided in this analysis, that what he is referring to may be considered a different concept altogether.

Alternatively, there are others who rather reject the notion of empathy and opt for a different interpretation to explain emotional response. Barratt (2006) proposes the "Associative Route" (2006:39) as a explanation which suggests evocation in film works in a system of cues and triggers which relies on "a lifetime of experience and the well-known Pavlovian process of classical conditioning" (ibid). That is to say, individuals who see or predict a stimulus in a film, much like in everyday life, respond in an automatic way established through previous experiences. However, although the theory of classical conditioning has garnered significant support in the field of psychology, the findings from this particular research project appear to be irreconcilable with such an approach. In the focus group discussion about *Pay It Forward* (2000), several participants, like Rachael below, were able to give specific details about why they felt emotionally moved by the film:

> …as it went on and as you learned [Trevor's] whole background and just the goodness in him, you were kind of just on his side the whole time and then it was just very shocking at the end and it was very sad.

Therefore, since participants were able to provide such certain details about why they felt emotionally impacted, then the unconscious processes required in Barratt's associative route appear to become secondary, if not irrelevant.

Frome (2006) also offers an approach which seeks to explore how individuals are able to respond emotively to the two separate worlds of actual life and a fictional narrative. It is referred to as the "Multi-Level Approach" (2006:14), and dates back to certain contradictions in emotion acknowledged by Plato in his piece, *The Republic* (380 BC). The premise of the theory states that "[w]e respond to representational media not with one overall judgment, but through multi-level appraisals, such that different mental systems evaluate them in different ways" (2006:15). Frome continues to explain that this approach has been applied to the context of film by Grodal (1997) who suggests there are two separate cognitive systems working simultaneously; local systems and global systems. Frome explains;

Crucially, the reality-status of things we perceive (i.e., whether they are real or representations) is determined by global appraisals. Global appraisals are determined by numerous local appraisals, which are limited evaluations, made by mental subsystems, that are not overall judgments about a situation. (2006:15)

Though difficult to prove with any degree of certainty, as a cognitive theory it does help account for divided emotional engagement which otherwise is an issue in this discussion. However, once again, the theory relies on unconscious mental processes to explain affective response, rather than allowing for the personal engagement of individual's to determine a response. Therefore, it also does not account for the variety, or in some cases, lack of response to fictional film. Interestingly, however, this topic regarding the variety of emotional response opens up an important discussion of the patterns involved in that process.

As part of this project's primary research, questionnaires were also presented to those who attended the screening of *Pay It Forward* (2000). One question sought to identify the participants' development of emotional investment, and interestingly, each participant provided the same answer; they all agreed that their emotional investment with the plot and characters increased incrementally as the film went on. The focus group then succeeded in identifying why this was, and once again they unanimously reported that they became more emotionally attached as they learned more about the characters and their backstories. This was clearly explained by Megan:

I think as you further understand the motivations of what they're doing and what it's like for them, about life for them and about how they see things and... why they are the way they are then you kind of feel more deeply for them.

Therefore, it has been established that a sense of closeness to fictional characters is developed as viewers learn more about them, and that empathy is significant to the acceptance of plot and characters but is not, by definition, an explanation for the full diversity of affective response. With these factors in mind, perhaps an alternative approach to the topic should be explored which takes these into account and offers a useful framework through which this project may be interpreted.

Film-viewing and Relationship

As previously mentioned, one of the assumptions made early in this research project supposed that in order to navigate the barrier between the real world and the fictional world of film, a specific set of human emotive processes would be required that differed from those which contribute to everyday relationships. However, considering empathy's apparent significance in both real life relationships as well as in the development of attachment to fictional characters, a more overlapping perspective could offer valuable insight into this topic as a whole. Neill (1996) refers to Kundera (1984) who emphasises the importance of compassion, and places this notion into the discussion of fiction; "Kundera's discourse on compassion, which is woven into his fictional narrative, illuminates... the possible scope of his readers' relationships to characters" (1996:184). It was this that first challenged the assumption that there must be a discrepancy between the emotive processes involved in viewing fiction film, and those involved in actual relationships.

Furthermore, interestingly, this project's primary research data supports the assertion that our affective response to film characters and events is not simply an unconscious byproduct of conditioning (Barratt, 2006) or an imitation of behaviour (Lipps, 1926), but rather a genuine care for even those who are fictional. As mentioned above, Rachael described being personally saddened by Trevor's death after having learned about him and come to relate with his goals, while Megan

12

expressed feeling deeply for characters for the same reason. Similarly, Clare, another participant, suggested "it doesn't matter what the plot is it's more about actually being able to feel what the character feels." All these statements reflect not just reactions of detached observers, but of active partners who are to some extent emotionally invested in the characters' lives. If this relational approach to understanding affective response to fictional film is indeed worth consideration, there are still important which remain unexplored. Firstly is detail into how such a relational approach is fostered; and secondly is the place, if any, for empathy within the theory which has otherwise been considered valuable.

Firstly, with regards to what this relational approach entails, perhaps an appropriate place to begin is in searching for parallels between the formation of actual relationships and the development of care for fictional characters. One significant likeness is in the process of disclosure which assumes different forms in both cases, but ultimately achieves the same goal. Christensen (2011), in referring to factors which contribute to the strengthening of friendship, states:

> Sensibly, the more that an individual reveals to a friend, the closer the bond between the two. In other words, the communicative practice of self-disclosure is imperative in the development and maintenance of a close friendship. (2011:1)

This appreciation for the importance of disclosure in friendship is echoed by many others, and if it is a strongly influential process in the formation of relationships, then it also favours the relational approach to affect and film. Returning once again to the case of *Pay It Forward* (2000), the viewer is presented with a backstory to the protagonist, Trevor, gradually throughout the film. The details revealed could be considered very personal and significant to his character. For example, we learn that his mother is a relapsing alcoholic who is struggling to provide for him with two jobs, and that his now absent father was also an abusive addict. If Trevor were a friend to a viewer in real life, a great deal of trust and closeness would be required, or gained, through the disclosure of such information; in the context of film, the disclosure occurs naturally.

It is also notable that affective response to film, as this research has revealed, is capable of lasting significantly longer than the duration of the film, or the event which the response is stimulated by. In the focus group Megan explained that, depending on the film, her emotional response can remain for considerable lengths of time; "[l]ike, until the next day sometimes. It really hits me hard. Like, I don't really know why that is but it can be a real emotional investment." The relational approach, unlike several other theories mentioned above which depend on emotional responses being only temporary, assumes that if a genuine care is built for characters that it would not fade so instantly.

The relevance of empathy is thus the final issue within this approach which emphasises the development of relationship between viewer and character as the most reasonable explanation for affective response. One of the problematic assumptions in beginning this project was in supposing emotional response to fictional character ought to be treated differently to the emotional dynamics at play in actual human relationship. However, if empathy is recognised as an important part of everyday relationships, and it is those relationships that form the framework of this analysis of affective response to film, then empathy may still occupy an important role in the process. As Neill (1996) remarks; "it is partly [empathy], I suggest, that gives film fiction its value: it gives us practice, so to speak, in a mode of engagement and response that is often crucial in our attempts to engage with and understand our fellow human beings" (1996:189).

Conclusion

Having provided an in-depth analysis of this project's focus, exploring the complexity of audience response alongside its diverse range of explanation with reference to primary research data, this discussion reaches its conclusion. The analysis began by outlining two problematic assumptions about empathy and emotion elicitation, and subsequently sought to critically engage with them. This outcome, therefore, intends to offer a more considered solution. Firstly, an inquiry into the capacity of empathy to account for the range of affective responses to film led instead to an admission of its limitations. Though it appeared to contribute heavily to a film-viewer's understanding and acceptance of plot and characters, it could not be justifiably regarded as the direct inciting cause of emotional expression. In turn, the recognition of this allowed for an openness to alternative explanations. Secondly, when the notion of empathy was first replaced with that of compassion (Kundera, 1984), the assumption that affect towards fictional characters is distinct from affect within real relationships was challenged. And so, it was through the valuing of both empathy and the notion of relationship between fiction and reality, that a final conclusion could be found. This conclusion is one which appreciates the role of empathy as active in contributing towards a sense of closeness with characters, just as it does in everyday relationships, and recognises the natural instinct of people to connect with others in such a way that the boundary of fiction makes little impact.

Bibliography

Barratt, D 2006 Tracing the Routes to Empathy: Association, Simulation, or Appraisal? *Film Studies* 8, no.1: 39-5

Basch, M.F 1983 Empathic understanding: A review of the concept and some theoretical considerations. *Journal of the American Psychoanalytic Association* 31:101-126

Carroll, N 1990 *The Philosophy of Horror, or Paradoxes of the Heart* New York: Routledge

Christensen, K 2011 "You're the Only Person I Can Talk To": The Role of Self-Disclosure in the Social Construction of Friendship. In *Journal of Undergraduate Research XIV*

Eisenstein, S 1991 *Towards a Theory of Montage: Sergei Eisenstein Selected Works 2* London: BFI

"Empathy" *Merriam-Webster.com* 2015. Internet document accessed 21/1/16 at http://www.merriam-webster.com/dictionary/empathy

Friedberg, A 1990 A Denial of Difference: Theories of Cinematic Identification. In *Psychoanalysis and Cinema* New York: Routledge

Frome, J 2006 'Representation, Reality, and Emotions Across Media'. *Film Studies* 8:12-25

Grodal, T 1997 *Moving Pictures: A New Theory of Film Genres, Feelings, and Cognition* Oxford: Clarendon Press

Grodal, T 2009 *Embodied Visions: Evolution, Emotion, Culture, and Film* Oxford: Oxford University Press

Grodal, T.K and M.Kramer 2010, 'Empathy, Film, and the Brain'. *Semiotic Inquiry* 30, no.1-2-3: 19-35

Kumar, R 2005 *Research Methodology: A Step-by-Step Guide for Beginners* SAGE publications

Kundera, M 1984 *The Unbearable Lightness of Being* New York: Harper & Row

Lipps, T 1926 *Psychological Studies* Baltimore, MD: Williams and Wilkens

Plantinga, C.R and Smith G.M 1999 *Passionate Views: Film, Cognition, and Emotion* Baltimore: The Johns Hopkins University Press

Plantinga, C.R 2006 Disgusted at the Movies. *Film Studies* 8, no.1: 81-92

Plantinga, C.R 2009 *Moving Viewers: American Film and the Spectator's Experience* California: University of California Press

Smith, G.M 2004 *Film Structure and the Emotion System* Cambridge: Cambridge University Press

Stoller, P 1989 *The Taste of Ethnographic Things: The Senses in Anthropology* Pensilvania: University of Pensilvania Press

Stotland, E., 1969. Exploratory Investigations of Empathy. *Advances in Experimental Social Psychology,* 4:271–314.

Swanger, D 1993 The Arts, Empathy, and Aristotle. *The Journal of Aesthetic Education* 27, no. 1:41-49

Neill, A 1996 Empathy and (film) fiction. In, Bordwell, D and Carroll, N *Post-Theory: Reconstructing Film Studies,* 175-194. Madison: University of Wisconsin Press

Metz, C 1982 *The Imaginary Signifier: Psychoanalysis and the Cinema* Indiana University Press

Pay It Forward 2000 dir. Mimi Leder

Toy Story 1995 dir. John Lassetter

Don't Look Now 1973 dir. Nicholas Roeg

YOUR KNOWLEDGE HAS VALUE

- We will publish your bachelor's and
  master's thesis, essays and papers

- Your own eBook and book -
  sold worldwide in all relevant shops

- Earn money with each sale

Upload your text at www.GRIN.com
and publish for free